SKILL BUILDER
GRAMMAR

LEVEL
4

PUFFIN BOOKS

An imprint of Penguin Random House

PUFFIN BOOKS

USA | Canada | UK | Ireland | Australia
New Zealand | India | South Africa | China

Puffin Books is part of the Penguin Random House group of companies
whose addresses can be found at global.penguinrandomhouse.com

Published by Penguin Random House India Pvt. Ltd
7th Floor, Infinity Tower C, DLF Cyber City,
Gurgaon 122 002, Haryana, India

First published in Puffin Books by Penguin Random House India 2021

Text, design and illustrations copyright © Quadrum Solutions Pvt. Ltd 2021
Series copyright © Penguin Random House India 2021

All rights reserved

10 9 8 7 6 5 4 3 2 1

ISBN 9780143445067

Design and layout by Quadrum Solutions Pvt. Ltd
Printed at Aarvee Promotions, India

www.penguin.co.in

Dear Moms and Dads,

There's no better way to prepare your children for their future than to equip them with all the skills they need to grow into confident adults. The Skill Builder series has been created to hone subject skills as well as twenty-first century skills so that children develop not just academic skills but also life skills.

The books in the Skill Builder series focus on numerical, science and English language skills. Recognizing that children learn best while having fun, the books in this series have been created with a high 'fun' quotient. Each subject is dealt with across four levels, so you can choose the level that best suits your child's learning stage.

The Skill Builder: Grammar books have been created by academic experts who have devised a special skill development chart to help you track the skills your child acquires as they complete the activities.

It has been great creating this series with my highly charged Quadrum team—our academic experts, Sutapa Sen and Naimisha Sanghavi, who spent hours crafting each page; Himani, who designed every page to be a visual treat; Kushal, who painstakingly laid out every number and sign; Bishnupriya and Ruby, who read and reread every word; and Kunjli, who was the conscience of the entire series. And of course, the Puffin team— Sohini and Ashwitha—who added value at every step. When you have a great team, you're bound to have a great book.

I do hope you and your child enjoy the series as much as we have enjoyed creating it.

Sonia Mehta
PS: We'd love your feedback, so do write in to us at

funlearningbooks@quadrumltd.com

THE SKILL CHART

Here's a snapshot of the skills your child will acquire as they complete the activities:

- **Reading skills:** The ability to read and comprehend text with proficiency.
- **Writing skills:** The ability to form meaningful sentences and write with proficiency.
- **Speaking skills:** The ability to speak fluently and proficiently in the English language.
- **Punctuation skills:** The ability to use punctuation marks in the correct manner so as to form meaningful sentences.
- **Creative thinking skills:** The ability to view a problem creatively from different angles.
- **Decision-making skills:** The ability to choose between possible solutions to a problem through an intuitive or reasoned process, or both.
- **Critical thinking/problem-solving skills:** Rationalizing, analysing, evaluating and interpreting information to make informed judgements.

Page no.		Reading	Writing	Speaking	Punctuation	Creative thinking	Decision-making	Problem-solving/ Critical thinking
4	COMPOUND THEM ALL	☺				☺	☺	☺
5	ALL SORTED	☺	☺			☺	☺	☺
6	PERFECT PHRASE	☺	☺			☺	☺	☺
7	THE RIGHT NOUN		☺					☺
8	PRONOUN MATCH	☺						☺
9	FILL THEM UP		☺			☺	☺	☺
10	JIGSAW JUGGLE	☺				☺	☺	☺
12	THINK LINK	☺						☺
13	MODAL MANIA		☺		☺	☺		
14	RATHER IRREGULAR		☺			☺	☺	☺
15	TICKED OFF		☺			☺	☺	☺
16	WHAT'S THE NOUN?	☺	☺					☺
17	WHAT'S THE ADJECTIVE?	☺	☺			☺		☺
18	FUN WITH SUFFIXES		☺		☺	☺		☺
20	ADJECTIVE HUNT					☺	☺	☺

COMPOUND THEM ALL

Match each word in Column A to an appropriate word in Column B to form compound nouns.

Column A

- rain
- break
- air
- tooth
- green
- news

Column B

- craft
- house
- bow
- paper
- fast
- paste

ALL SORTED

Here are some sets of words that form compound words when put together. Rewrite each set in its correct form in the appropriate column. One has been done for you.

Tip: Remember to add hyphens wherever needed.

basket ball	passer by	thunder storm
swimming pool	bed time	blood pressure
down stairs	runners up	bath room
pass word	bottle opener	ice cream
traffic jam	daughter in law	post office

Closed	**Separated**	**Hyphenated**
(One word)	(Two words)	(Joined by a hyphen)
basketball		

PERFECT PHRASE

Choose an appropriate collective noun from the box to complete each phrase below. One has been done for you.

collection   army   bunch   sheaf   chest   string
fleet   band   crew   library   kennel   gang

1   a [bunch] of keys   7   a [   ] of musicians

2   a [   ] of books   8   a [   ] of dogs

3   a [   ] of cars   9   a [   ] of thieves

4   a [   ] of paper   10   an [   ] of ants

5   a [   ] of drawers   11   a [   ] of sailors

6   a [   ] of coins   12   a [   ] of pearls

THE RIGHT NOUN

Use appropriate collective nouns to complete these sentences.

1. I saw a [_____] of puppies at Harini's house.

2. We presented Mrs Sanchez with a [_____] of flowers.

3. He took the [_____] of cattle out to graze.

4. Sam took a picture of the hen with her [_____] of chicks.

5. My grandpa climbed the [_____] of stairs very slowly.

6. The houses collapsed like a [_____] of cards.

7. The [_____] of sheep made their way across the meadow.

PRONOUN MATCH

Match the personal pronouns on the left to the reflexive pronouns on the right.

Tip: Remember, a reflexive pronoun is used to refer to the doer or subject of a sentence.

I •	• ourselves
you (singular) •	• himself
we •	• itself
he •	• myself
she •	• themselves
it •	• yourself
they •	• yourselves
you (plural) •	• herself

8

FILL THEM UP

Fill in the blanks with appropriate pronouns from the box.

> herself   he   she   you   ourselves   they   it
> themselves   himself   myself   me   yourself

1   Varun told his sister that [_____] would not be able to go to the doctor with her. She would have to go by [_____].

2   Diana did not buy the dress as [_____] was expensive.

3   Diego, Maya and the others decided that [_____] would divide up the winnings among [_____].

4   Mum said that the fruits were for the guests, but we ate them [_____].

5   Robin is quite clumsy. [_____] keeps injuring [_____].

JIGSAW JUGGLE

One word is missing in each sentence. Find the puzzle piece that contains the missing word. Then, colour the pieces that go together using the same colour crayon. One has been done for you.

Lisa _____ cooked for all the guests.

itself

himself

He tried to kick the ball hard but hurt _____.

Do your homework by _____.

themselves

The students prepared _____ for the talent contest.

We blamed _____ for not completing the project on time.

The monkey was scared when it found _____ in a cage.

herself

ourselves

yourself

myself

I ate the entire cake all by _____.

THINK LINK

Fill in the blanks with appropriate linking verbs from the box.

has been	were	are	have been	is	was	will be

1. Jay _____ happy with his grades last year.

2. Neel _____ absent today as he is not well.

3. Amina, you _____ disturbing the other students.

4. The oceans _____ filling up with plastic rubbish for a long time.

5. I _____ joining the theatre group this week.

6. They _____ all present for the ceremony yesterday.

7. It _____ very cold since yesterday.

MODAL MANIA

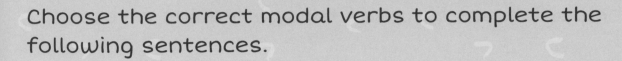

Choose the correct modal verbs to complete the following sentences.

1   _____ Could/Can you please help me open this jar of pickle?

2   My grandfather _____ could/can remember all our telephone numbers when he was younger but not any more.

3   I _____ shall/should be at the theatre at 7.00 p.m.

4   The concert was amazing. You _____ shall/should have been there.

5   Mum asked, 'Which book _____ will/would you like to read before bed tonight, Sam?'

6   John says he _____ will/would go trekking next weekend.

7   Look at those grey clouds. It _____ may/might rain today.

8   _____ May/Would I have some ice cream after dinner?

RATHER IRREGULAR

Write the past tense forms of these irregular verbs.

be | have | do | come

get | say | make | hear

go | see | tell | smell

TICKED OFF

Tick (✔) the correct past tense forms for these irregular verbs.

1. begin | ( ) begined | ( ) began | ( ) begun
2. catch | ( ) catched | ( ) catching | ( ) caught
3. hurt | ( ) hurt | ( ) hurted | ( ) hurting
4. slide | ( ) slide | ( ) slid | ( ) slod
5. creep | ( ) crept | ( ) creeped | ( ) creeping
6. learn | ( ) learned | ( ) learnt | ( ) learn
7. fling | ( ) flung | ( ) flang | ( ) flanged
8. wind | ( ) wound | ( ) winded | ( ) wounded

WHAT'S THE NOUN?

Write the noun forms of these adjectives. One has been done for you.

Adjectives

anxious

curious

jealous

painful

wise

lucky

warm

responsible

Nouns

anxiety

WHAT'S THE ADJECTIVE?

Write the adjective forms of these verbs. One has been done for you.

Verbs	Adjectives
bore →	boring
admire →	
confuse →	
destroy →	
envy →	
smile →	
lose →	
whiten →	

FUN WITH SUFFIXES

Use the appropriate suffixes from the box to convert each adjective into a noun. Then, make a sentence using both the noun and the adjective forms of each word.

| -ness | -ity | -ment | -ence | -ance |

happy

_____

_____

scarce

_____

_____

18

merry

_____

_____

silent

_____

_____

appear

_____

_____

ADJECTIVE HUNT

Find the adjective forms of the following verbs in the grid below.

amuse   attract   care   glorify

courage   inform   narrow

comfort   irritate   observe

E	S	I	R	R	I	T	A	T	I	N	G	X	G	A
A	R	A	C	X	M	F	Y	E	L	N	F	X	L	H
X	S	P	O	H	L	O	A	G	K	T	H	A	O	Q
U	X	S	U	C	P	B	T	H	R	A	Y	M	R	R
M	I	A	R	O	S	S	T	H	L	B	I	U	I	N
Z	W	D	A	M	N	E	R	S	E	H	H	S	O	A
R	K	O	G	F	V	R	A	C	O	L	O	I	U	R
Y	S	P	E	O	U	V	C	E	W	F	E	N	S	R
I	N	F	O	R	M	A	T	I	V	E	S	G	L	O
F	T	V	U	T	C	N	I	C	E	O	L	A	I	W
D	I	D	S	A	J	T	V	R	N	H	P	J	U	W
I	D	N	H	B	F	G	E	D	M	Y	B	Q	P	M
C	Q	J	O	L	I	Q	Y	M	J	Z	K	S	J	G
I	H	X	N	E	T	Z	H	V	F	N	Q	A	E	Z
Y	J	Y	C	A	R	E	F	U	L	Y	N	O	O	L

20

SORT THEM OUT

Rewrite each word in the correct column.
One has been done for you.

amazed   annoyance   cheerful   food
deafness   consider   hopeful   pleasant
see   ownership   fascinating   growth
modernity   perform   include   national
delight   belief   accept   education
educate   crazy   inventive

Nouns	Verbs	Adjectives
	amazed	

LET'S COMPARE

Use the comparative form of the highlighted adjective to complete each sentence. One has been done for you.

1 Onions are [costlier] than potatoes. cost

2 Gold is [   ] than silver. expensive

3 My shirt is a [   ] colour than Sam's. dark

4 Mira is [   ] than Tina. quick

5 This painting is [   ] than that one. beautiful

6 Cricket is [   ] than football in India. popular

7 Mumbai is a [   ] city than Kolkata. busy

CORRECT THEM ALL

The comparatives in these sentences are all wrong.
Rewrite each sentence to be correct.

1   Arav is gooder at sports than Sunny.

_____

2   Jo ran far than me.

_____

3   Edgar is eagerer to learn martial arts than Tito.

_____

4   My sculpture is worser than Sheena's.

_____

5   I would like to improver my knowledge of astronomy.

_____

DO THE DEGREE

Complete this paragraph using the correct forms of the highlighted adjectives.

My brother Eric returned from London today after completing his degree. We are three siblings—Eric, Diana and I. Eric is the _____ old . We were all excited about his return, but my grandmother was the _____ happy of all. Eric has always been her favourite. Mum asked me to bake a cheesecake, but I requested Diana to make it as she is a _____ good baker than me.
When Eric arrived, he exclaimed, 'Hey! You have grown _____ tall than me, but Dad is still the _____ tall of us all.' We gathered around him and chatted gleefully. He handed Diana a package and said, 'This is for my _____ little sister.'
'Thank you, Eric!' She opened the package and said happily, 'How did you know I wanted this book? This is way _____ good than that stupid dress you brought me the last time you visited.' Eric then handed me my package. I opened it excitedly. It was the _____ big encylopedia I had ever seen! I hugged Eric and thanked him.

ADVERB COMPARE

Use the correct degree of comparison for the highlighted adverbs to complete the sentences.

1. Amit bowls [_____] fast than Andrew.

2. Sonia can solve puzzles [_____] quickly than me.

3. We should try to use electricity [_____] efficiently than we do right now.

4. Dad visits Grandma [_____] often than he used to before.

5. He shouted [_____] loudly than the other children.

6. Sunil hit the ball [_____] powerfully than he thought he could.

COMPARATIVELY CORRECT

Write the comparative degree of the following adverbs. Then, make a sentence using both forms of the adverb.

badly

early

little

_____

_____

much

_____

_____

well

_____

_____

TAG IT

Match the sentences on the left to the appropriate question tags.

You are angry,	don't I?
He wasn't at the store,	should he?
They have won the last game,	mustn't he?
I like chocolate,	isn't he?
Barry must see a doctor,	can't he?
Jimmy shouldn't be doing that,	was he?
Uncle Omar is amazing,	aren't you?
Dev can play the electric drum,	haven't they?

BAG THE TAG

Rewrite the following sentences using the correct question tags and punctuation.

1   Sunny and Shaila witnessed the accident.

_____

2   The students haven't received their identity cards.

_____

3   She said she would do some gardening.

_____

4   My uncle doesn't eat fish.

_____

5   You can take the groceries home.

_____

TAGS ARE FUN, AREN'T THEY?

Underline the errors in these sentences. Then, rewrite the sentences correctly in the space provided.

1   We didn't play the match, haven't we?

_____

2   They haven't done their lessons, aren't they?

_____

3   She did believe me, did she?

_____

4   Neal is from Canada, wasn't he?

_____

5   This box is made of wood, isn't they?

_____

PERFECTLY PREFIXED

Match the prefixes in the yellow wheel to the words in the blue wheel to make new words. Write your new words in the boxes below.

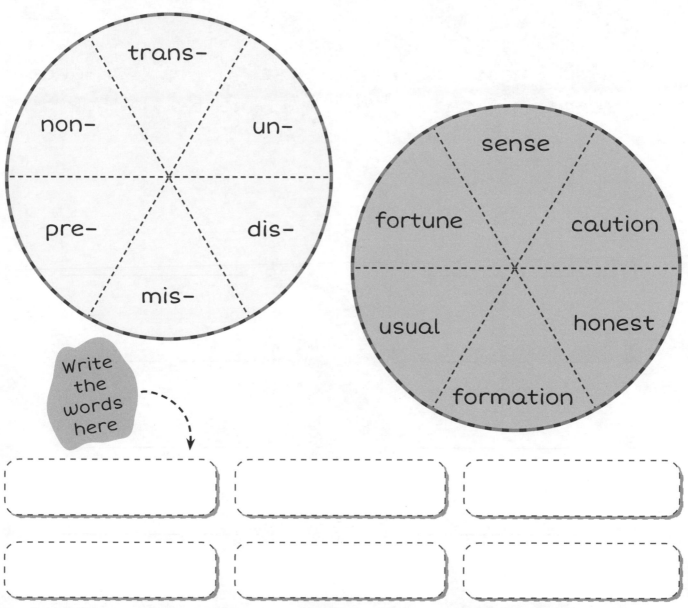

trans-

non-

un-

pre-

dis-

mis-

sense

fortune

caution

usual

honest

formation

Write the words here

SUPER SUFFIXES

Use the suffixes in the box to make eight words. You cannot use the same suffix more than once!

-able   -ness   -ful   -like   -ity   -ance

-ence   -age   -ian   -ment   -tude

1 _____

2 _____

3 _____

4 _____

5 _____

6 _____

7 _____

8 _____

BEGINNING AND END

Basket A contains root words and Basket B contains prefixes and suffixes. Match the words in Basket A to a prefix or a suffix from Basket B to make as many new words as you can!

Basket A

responsible
order
tiger
behave
magic
involve
care
legal
possible
ordinary
reversible
cast
refer
assist

Basket B

ir-   -ity
-ian
extra-
mis-
-ment
il-
-ant
im-
-ess
dis-
-ence
fore-
-less

Write the words here

SMART SIMILES

Can you complete the following common similes?
Tip: The clue is in the images!

1 That baby is as cute as a _____.

2 No one can beat Emma in a race. She is as quick as _____.

3 My mother is always as busy as a _____.

4 Ajay looked timid but was as brave as a _____ with the miscreants.

5 My little niece is as playful as a _____.

6 Tanya was as cold as _____ when I tried to talk to her.

FIGURE IT OUT

Explain the metaphors in the following sentences.
One has been done for you.

1　My grandfather is a walking dictionary.

My grandfather knows the meanings of a lot of words.

2　My aunt has a heart of gold.

_____

3　The sound of the waves is music to my ears.

_____

4　The garden has become a jungle.

_____

5　Jackie is the shining star of our generation.

_____

SIMILE OR METAPHOR?

Circle 'S' if the sentence has a simile and 'M' if it has a metaphor.

1. My mother is my guardian angel.
   S | M

2. They fought like cats and dogs.
   S | M

3. Brett has been decorating his new house. He has been as busy as a beaver.
   S | M

4. Lina cut him down to size with her harsh words.
   S | M

5. After the exams were over, Sally felt as light as a feather.
   S | M

6. Anne's expression turned wooden when she heard the bad news.
   S | M

7. Even in the most difficult situations, Ronny is as cool as a cucumber.
   S | M

8. The clouds sailed across the sky.
   S | M

PERSONIFIED WORDS

Underline the words or phrases that indicate personification. One has been done for you.

1   Opportunity does not **knock** twice.

2   The tsunami gobbled up entire villages along the coast.

3   Moonlight peeped through the window into Eric's bedroom.

4   The last slice of cake called out to me.

5   The gloomy, grey clouds filled the sky and blocked out the sun.

6   My alarm yells at me at 7.00 a.m. every day.

7   The paddy fields swayed to and fro in the gentle breeze.

8   The thunder's roar frightened Mary terribly.

TWO BECOME ONE

Rewrite each pair of simple sentences into a compound sentence using appropriate connectors.

1   It is not raining. The sky is clear.

_____

2   It was dark in the woods. They had lost their way.

_____

3   I did not want to visit a dentist. I had to go
     because I had a toothache.

_____

4   There was no chocolate at home. They
     went to the store to get some.

_____

COMPLEX CRACKER

Make complex sentences by matching the sentence fragments in Column A to appropriate ones in Column B.

Column A

- Even after Peter had graduated
- Although Gopal is a good batsman
- For as long she was in the room
- After my parents had agreed to listen
- When Grandpa telephoned us
- So long as we had no news

Column B

- I told them what I wanted to do with my life.
- we could not help imagining the worst.
- he often went back to visit his teachers.
- he is working on his bowling.
- Miranda did not leave Joe's side.
- we had just sat down to dinner.

COMPOUND VS COMPLEX

Circle the correct box to say whether each of these sentences is compound or complex.

1. If you want to come with me, you have to be ready on time.

   compound | complex

2. While you were away, your mother tidied up your study.

   compound | complex

3. She did not take the test as she had not prepared for it.

   compound | complex

4. Since the food had grown cold, I heated it up in the microwave.

   compound | complex

5. I thought I would get the prize, but Harry got it instead.

   compound | complex

6. Everyone was busy, so I had to go by myself to my computer class.

   compound | complex

7. When our team finally won the game, we jumped for joy.

   compound | complex

8. Dogs are excellent pets, for they are loving and faithful.

   compound | complex

BEING NEGATIVE

Use negative words from the box to answer the following questions. One has been done for you.

> no   not   never   none   nobody   neither   nor

1   Is there a train that leaves at 6.00 p.m.?

   No, there is no train that leaves at 6.00 p.m.

2   Has Max ever been to London?

   _____

3   Do you think Ami or Ali will want to come with us?

   _____

4   Has anybody been to this shop recently?

   _____

5   Does Sharan play the piano these days?

   _____

TIME FOR CHANGE

Transform these positive sentences into negative sentences without changing their meanings.

1   The farmer was too feeble to speak.

_____

2   Jenny can drive faster than Tom.

_____

3   These books are quite cheap.

_____

4   All the students liked the story.

_____

Now, change these positive sentences into negative sentences using negative phrases.

Hint: The meaning will change.

1   The furniture was in the garage.

_____

2   Uma spoke to her teacher.

_____

3   The children wanted to play games all afternoon.

_____

4   She will sing a song during the concert.

_____

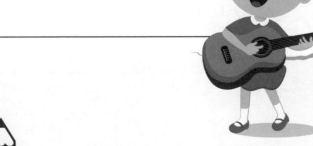

SO THAT'S THE TASK

Find the incorrect sentences and rewrite them using 'so . . . that'.

1   I woke up early because I can go for a walk.

_____

2   I need a raincoat to stay dry in the rain.

_____

3   She bought a needle because she mend the tear in her dress.

_____

4   Firoze worked very hard because he could get the grades he needed.

_____

5   I read the newspaper every day because I know the latest news.

_____

REPORT THE SPEECH

Rewrite these sentences to be in direct speech.

Hint: Punctuate the sentences appropriately.

1   My father said that he will be going to Dubai next week.

    _____

2   They said that they are ready to start the meeting.

    _____

3   Graeme said that he had not read the book.

    _____

4   My friend said that she went to the park.

    _____

5   Mira said that she does not like pasta.

    _____

CONNECTING SENTENCES

Connect each pair of sentences using 'not only . . . but also'.

1. He eats vegetables. He eats meat.

   _____

2. My mother is a teacher. She helps with the household chores.

   _____

3. I have done my maths homework. I have done my history homework.

   _____

4. Her father was angry with her. He was disappointed by her behaviour.

   _____

5   Scott plays football well. He is good at maths.

_____

6   You need to drink a lot of liquids. You need to rest
to get better.

_____

7   Simi is acting in the play. She is designing the stage.

_____

8   Paul and Pablo play together. They study together.

_____

9   Ananya and Anne live in the same building. They go
to the same school.

_____

ACTIVE OR PASSIVE

Circle the correct box to say whether the following sentences are in active voice or passive voice.

1. Smith scored the winning run.

   active | passive

2. The concert was enjoyed by everyone.

   active | passive

3. Japan was struck by an earthquake last night.

   active | passive

4. This bottle contains oil.

   active | passive

5. I kept my word.

   active | passive

6. My earrings were snatched by a thief yesterday.

   active | passive

7. He gave me a letter.

   active | passive

8. Her singing was loved by her fans.

   active | passive

Rewrite each sentence in active voice so that it is in passive voice and vice versa.

1 _____

2 _____

3 _____

4 _____

5 _____

6 _____

7 _____

8 _____

PUNCTUATION FUN

Rewrite the paragraph adding articles, commas, semicolons and colons where necessary.

My uncle was finally coming home after a long expedition to Antarctica so we had a grand dinner planned for him. There are four of us My father mother elder sister Ira and me. My father decided to bake a cake Ira took charge of the appetizers and I was put in charge of cleaning the living room. The appetizers we had were stuffed mushrooms fish fingers and tomato soup. My mother cooked the main course which was fried rice roasted lemon chicken and baked cauliflower. Uncle Dan arrived right on time we gathered around him to hear all about about his adventures in Antarctica. He had a team of five people. All of them were Japanese. Team almost didn't reach Antarctica but they managed to make it in the end

Rewrite
here

CONTINUOUSLY PERFECT

Fill in the blanks with the present perfect continuous form of the highlighted verbs.

1 How long _____ you _____ teach at this school?

2 He _____ write letters all day.

3 I _____ create designs for my aunt's boutique since I was in college.

4 We _____ wait for you since six o'clock.

5 I think you are unwell as you _____ sleep for twelve hours.

6 They _____ not practise much for their game.

7 You _____ not drink enough water.

A CONTINUOUS PAST

Use the past perfect continuous forms of these verbs in sentences of your own.

learn   play   buy   run   study   say   call   move

_____

_____

_____

_____

_____

_____

_____

REPORT INDIRECTLY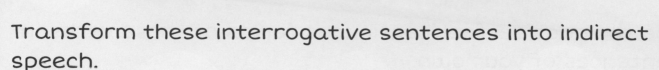

Transform these interrogative sentences into indirect speech.

Hint: Remember to punctuate correctly while changing the sentences.

1 'Aaron, why are you not studying?' asked Jasmine.

_____

_____

2 Jack asked, 'Where are you going, John?'

_____

_____

3 Bashir asked, 'Is your uncle a doctor?'

_____

_____

4 She asked, 'Can you help me?'

_____

_____

5   Pari asked, 'Who is this stranger with you, Don?'

_____

6   'What are you doing outside at night?' demanded the policeman.

_____

7   'When do you get up in the morning?' asked Sarah.

_____

8   Soli asked, 'Sheila, where is my computer?'

_____

9   'Can you please help me bake this cake?' asked Seema.

_____

STORY TIME

It is a cold winter evening and you are alone at home. Suddenly, you hear a knock at the door. A mysterious stranger stands outside.

Continue this story in any way you like!

Here are some reflexive pronouns, modal verbs, irregular verbs, question tags and metaphors you can use in your story.

reflexive pronouns	myself, himself, themselves
modals	can/could, may/might, should, must
irregular verbs	said, came, had, crept
question tags	aren't you, isn't it, haven't you
metaphors or similes	the wind was a howling wolf, as cold as ice, fear like black clouds

_____

_____

_____

PICTURE PERFECT

Write a description of what you see in this picture. Use compound nouns, reflexive pronouns, modal verbs, adjectives formed from nouns and comparative adverbs in your description.

EXIT

TOILET

_____

_____

ANSWERS

page 4 COMPOUND THEM ALL

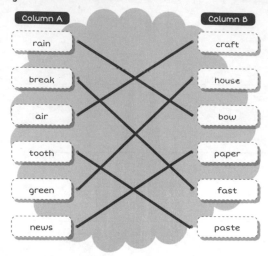

Column A	Column B
rain	craft
break	house
air	bow
tooth	paper
green	fast
news	paste

page 5 ALL SORTED
Closed: thunderstorm, bedtime, downstairs, bathroom, password, passerby
Separated: swimming pool, post office, blood pressure, bottle opener, traffic jam, ice cream
Hyphenated: runners-up, daughter-in-law

page 6 PERFECT PHRASE
2. library; 3. fleet; 4. sheaf; 5. chest; 6. collection;
7. band; 8. kennel; 9. gang; 10. army; 11. crew; 12. string

page 7 THE RIGHT NOUN
1. litter; 2. bouquet/bunch; 3. herd; 4. brood; 5. flight; 6. pack;
7. flock

page 8 PRONOUN MATCH

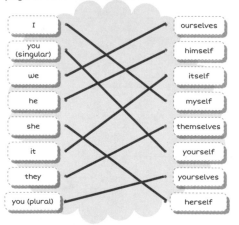

I	ourselves
you (singular)	himself
we	itself
he	myself
she	themselves
it	yourself
they	yourselves
you (plural)	herself

page 9 FILL THEM UP
1. he, herself; 2. it; 3. they, themselves; 4. ourselves;
5. He OR She, himself OR herself

pages 10–11 JIGSAW JUGGLE
Lisa herself cooked for all the guests.
Do your homework by yourself.
He tried to kick the ball hard but hurt himself.
The students prepared themselves for the talent contest.
We blamed ourselves for not completing the project on time.
The monkey was scared when it found itself in a cage.
I ate the entire cake all by myself.

page 12 THINK LINK
1. was; 2. is; 3. are; 4. have been; 5. will be; 6. were;
7. has been

page 13 MODAL MANIA
1. Could; 2. could; 3. shall; 4. should; 5. would; 6. will; 7. might;
8. May

page 14 RATHER IRREGULAR
was; had; did; came; got; said; made; heard; went; saw; told;
smelled

page 15 TICKED OFF
1. began; 2. caught; 3. hurt; 4. slid; 5. crept; 6. learnt (Please note that 'learned' is widely used as the past tense form of 'learn' in the US.); 7. flung; 8. wound

page 16 WHAT'S THE NOUN?
curiosity; jealousy; pain; wisdom; luck; warmth; responsibility

page 17 WHAT'S THE ADJECTIVE?
admirable; confused/confusing; destructive; envious; smiling; lost; white

pages 18–19 FUN WITH SUFFIXES
happiness; scarcity; merriment; silence; appearance
Sentences will vary.

page 20 ADJECTIVE HUNT

E	S	I	R	R	I	T	A	T	I	N	G	X	G	A
A	R	A	C	X	M	F	Y	E	L	N	F	X	L	H
X	S	P	O	H	L	O	A	G	K	T	H	A	O	Q
U	X	S	U	C	P	B	T	H	R	A	Y	M	R	R
M	I	A	R	O	S	S	T	H	L	B	I	U	I	N
Z	W	D	A	M	N	E	R	S	E	H	H	S	O	A
R	K	O	G	F	V	R	A	C	O	L	O	I	U	R
Y	S	P	E	O	U	V	C	E	W	F	E	N	S	R
I	N	F	O	R	M	A	T	I	V	E	S	G	L	O
F	T	V	U	T	C	N	I	C	E	O	L	A	I	W
D	I	D	S	A	J	T	V	R	N	H	P	J	U	W
I	D	N	B	F	G	E	D	M	Y	B	Q	P	M	
C	Q	J	O	L	I	Q	Y	M	J	Z	K	S	J	G
I	H	X	N	E	T	Z	H	V	F	N	Q	A	E	Z
Y	J	J	Y	C	A	R	E	F	U	L	Y	N	O	O	L

page 21 SORT THEM OUT

Nouns	Verbs	Adjectives
annoyance	amazed	cheerful
food	consider	hopeful
deafness	see	pleasant
ownership	delight	fascinating
growth	include	national
modernity	perform	crazy
belief	accept	inventive
education	educate	

page 22 LET'S COMPARE
2. more expensive; 3. darker; 4. quicker; 5. more beautiful;
6. more popular; 7. busier

page 23 CORRECT THEM ALL
1. Arav is better at sports than Sunny. 2. Jo ran farther than
me. 3. Edgar is more eager to learn martial arts than Tito.
4. My sculpture is worse than Sheena's. 5. I would like to
improve my knowledge of astronomy.

page 24 DO THE DEGREE
eldest; happiest; better; taller; tallest; little; better; biggest

page 25 ADVERB COMPARE
1. faster; 2. more quickly; 3. more efficiently; 4. more often;
5. more loudly; 6. more powerfully

pages 26—27 COMPARATIVELY CORRECT
worse; earlier; less; more; better
Sentences will vary.

page 28 TAG IT

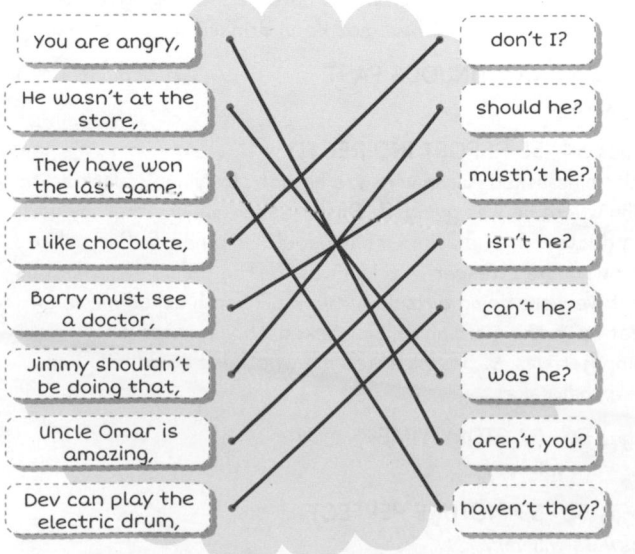

page 29 BAG THE TAG
1. Sunny and Shaila witnessed the accident, didn't they?
2. The students haven't received their identity cards, have
they? 3. She said she would do some gardening, didn't she?
4. My uncle doesn't eat fish, does he? 5. You can take the
groceries home, can't you?

page 30 TAGS ARE FUN, AREN'T THEY?
1. We didn't play the match, did we? 2. They haven't done their
lessons, have they? 3. She did believe me, didn't she?
4. Neal is from Canada, isn't he? 5. This box is made of wood,
isn't it?

page 31 PERFECTLY PREFIXED
unusual; dishonest; misfortune; transformation; precaution;
nonsense

page 32 SUPER SUFFIXES
Answers will vary.

page 33 BEGINNING AND END
disorder; misbehave; illegal; impossible; irreversible;
extraordinary; forecast; assistant; reference; tigress;
involvement; careless; responsibility; magician

page 34 SMART SIMILES
1. button; 2. lightning; 3. bee; 4. lion; 5. kitten; 6. ice

page 35 FIGURE IT OUT
2. My aunt is kind-hearted. 3. The sound of the waves is
pleasing to me. 4. The garden is growing wild like a jungle.
5. Jackie stands out as a remarkable person.

page 36 SIMILE OR METAPHOR?
1. M; 2. S; 3. S; 4. M; 5. S; 6. M; 7. S; 8. M

page 37 PERSONIFIED WORDS
2. gobbled up; 3. peeped; 4. called out; 5. gloomy, blocked out;
6. yells; 7. swayed; 8. roar

page 38 TWO BECOME ONE
1. It is not raining and the sky is clear. 2. It was dark in the
woods and they had lost their way. 3. I did not want to visit a
dentist, but I had to go because I had a toothache.
4. There was no chocolate at home, so they went to the store
to get some.

page 39 COMPLEX CRACKER

Column A	Column B
Even after Peter had graduated	I told them what I wanted to do with my life.
Although Gopal is a good batsman	we could not help imagining the worst.
After my parents had agreed to listen	he often went back to visit his teachers.
When Grandpa telephoned us	he is working on his bowling.
So long as we had no news	Miranda did not leave Joe's side.
For as long as she was in the room	we had just sat down to dinner.

page 40 COMPOUND VS COMPLEX

1. complex; 2. complex; 3. compound; 4. complex; 5. compound; 6. compound; 7. complex; 8. compound

page 41 BEING NEGATIVE

2. Max has never been to London. 3. Neither Ami nor Ali will want to come with us. 4. Nobody has been to this shop recently. 5. No, Sharan does not play the piano these days.

pages 42-43 TIME FOR CHANGE

1. The farmer was so feeble that he could not speak. 2. Tom cannot drive as fast as Jenny. 3. These books are not expensive. 4. The students did not dislike the story.

1. The furniture was not in the garage. 2. Uma did not speak to her teacher. 3. The children did not want to play games all afternoon. 4. She will not sing a song during the concert.

page 44 SO THAT'S THE TASK

1. I woke up early so that I could go for a walk. 2. I need a raincoat so that I stay dry in the rain. 3. She bought a needle so that she could mend the tear in her dress. 4. Firoze worked very hard so that he could get the grades he needed. 5. I read the newspaper every day so that I know the latest news.

page 45 REPORT THE SPEECH

1. My father said, 'I will be going to Dubai next week.' 2. They said, 'We are ready to start the meeting.' 3. Graeme said, 'I have not read the book.' 4. My friend said, 'I went to the park.' 5. Mira said, 'I do not like pasta.'

pages 46-47 CONNECTING SENTENCES

1. He eats not only vegetables but also meat. 2. My mother is not only a teacher but she also helps with the household chores. 3. I have not only done my maths homework, but also my history homework. 4. Her father was not only angry with her but also disappointed by her behaviour. 5. Scott not only plays football well but he is also good at maths. 6. Not only do you need to drink a lot of liquids but you also need to rest to get better. 7. Simi is not only acting in the play but also designing the stage. 8. Paul and Pablo not only play together but also study together. 9. Ananya and Anne not only live in the same building but also go to the same school.

pages 48-49 ACTIVE OR PASSIVE

1. active; 2. passive; 3. passive; 4. active; 5. active; 6. passive; 7. active; 8. passive;

1. The winning run was scored by Smith. 2. Everyone enjoyed the concert. 3. An earthquake struck Japan last night. 4. Oil is contained in the bottle. 5. My word was kept. 6. A thief snatched my earrings yesterday. 7. The letter was given to me by him. 8. Her fans loved her singing.

pages 50-51 PUNCTUATION FUN

My uncle was finally coming home after a long expedition to Antarctica, so we had a grand dinner planned for him. There are four of us: my father, mother, elder sister Ira and me. My father decided to bake a cake; Ira took charge of the appetizers and I was put in charge of cleaning the living room. The appetizers we had were stuffed mushrooms, fish fingers and tomato soup. My mother cooked the main course, which was fried rice, roasted lemon chicken and baked cauliflower. Uncle Dan arrived right on time. We gathered around him to hear all about his adventures in Antarctica. He had a team of five people. All of them were Japanese. The team almost didn't reach Antarctica, but they managed to make it in the end.

page 52 CONTINUOUSLY PERFECT

1. have been teaching; 2. has been writing; 3. have been creating; 4. have been waiting; 5. have been sleeping; 6. have been practising; 7. have not been drinking

page 53 A CONTINUOUS PAST

Answers will vary.

pages 54-55 REPORT INDIRECTLY

1. Jasmine asked Aaron why he was not studying. 2. Jack asked John where he was going. 3. Bashir asked me whether my uncle is a doctor. 4. She asked me if I could help her. 5. Pari asked Don who the stranger with him was. 6. The policeman asked us what we were doing outside at night. 7. Sarah asked me when I get up in the morning. 8. Soli asked Sheila where his computer was. 9. Seema asked me whether I could help her bake that cake.

pages 56-57 STORY TIME

Answers will vary.

pages 58-59 PICTURE PERFECT

Answers will vary.